Pioneer Spirit
The
Westward
Expansion

THE GOLD RUSH

Rachel Lynette

PowerKiDS press

New Yor—

For my Dad

Published in 2014 by The Rosen Publishing Group, Inc.
29 East 21st Street, New York, NY 10010

First Edition

Editor: Jennifer Way
Book Design: Greg Tucker

Photo Credits: Cover, p. 8 Stock Montage/Archive Photos/Getty Images; p. 5 SuperStock/Getty Images; p. 6 National Archives; p. 7 Interim Archives/Archive Photos/Getty Images; p. 9 © North Wind Picture Archives; p. 10 optimarc/Shutterstock.com; p. 11 © SuperStock/SuperStock; p. 13 © Corbis; p. 14 Timothy H. O'Sullivan/Hulton Archive/Getty Images; p. 15 Gary Saxe/Shutterstock.com; p. 17 American School/The Bridgeman Art Library/Getty Images; p. 18 Comstock/Thinkstock; p. 19 Fotosearch/Stringer/Archive Photos/Getty Images; p. 21 Underwood Archives/Archive Photos/Getty Images; p. 22 MPI/Stringer/Archive Photos/Getty Images.

Library of Congress Cataloging-in-Publication Data

Lynette, Rachel.
 The Gold Rush / by Rachel Lynette. — First edition.
     pages cm. — (Pioneer spirit: the westward expansion)
 Includes index.
 ISBN 978-1-4777-0784-5 (library binding) — ISBN 978-1-4777-0901-6 (pbk.) —
ISBN 978-1-4777-0902-3 (6-pack)
 1. California—Gold discoveries—Juvenile literature. 2. California—History—1846–1850—Juvenile literature. 3. Frontier and pioneer life—California--Juvenile literature. I. Title.
 F865.L975 2014
 979.4'04—dc23
                                2012049053

Manufactured in the United States of America

CONTENTS

An American Dream

In the early 1800s, not many American settlers lived in California. Like the rest of the West, the area was growing slowly. Then, in 1848, gold was discovered. Gold fever quickly spread across the United States and even to other countries. Soon thousands of people were flooding into California with dreams of finding enough gold to make themselves rich. By 1855, the Gold Rush was over.

The Gold Rush played a big role in **westward expansion**. Westward expansion was the movement of people from the eastern part of the United States to the West. Because of the Gold Rush, California grew very quickly in both **population** and wealth.

The Gold Rush drew many new settlers to California. Some crossed the country in covered wagons like the ones in this painting.

An Amazing Discovery

John Sutter came to the United States from Switzerland in 1834. He settled in the Sacramento Valley in what is now California. In 1841, the US government granted land to Sutter. He built a fort and hired people to farm his land.

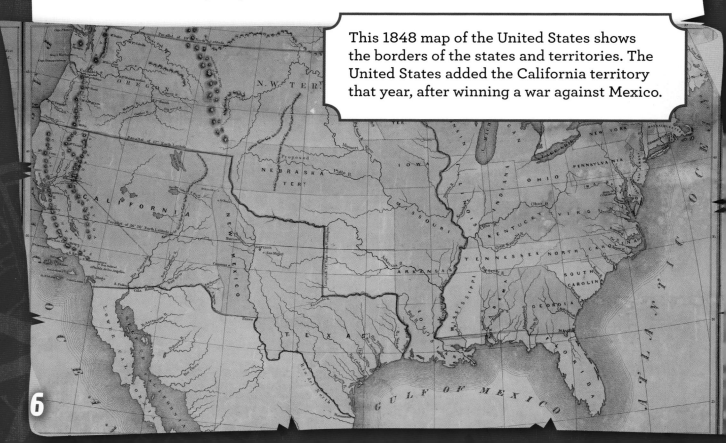

This 1848 map of the United States shows the borders of the states and territories. The United States added the California territory that year, after winning a war against Mexico.

John Sutter's land was known as Sutter's Mill. It was in Coloma, a little more than 100 miles (161 km) northeast of San Francisco. This picture shows Sutter's Mill in 1849, just after gold was discovered.

Sutter also hired people to build a **sawmill** on the American River. He hired a carpenter named James Marshall to lead the project. On January 24, 1848, Marshall saw something shiny in the river. It was gold! He showed the tiny nuggets to Sutter. Sutter wanted to keep the discovery a secret, but soon more of the workers found gold too.

Spreading the News

A storeowner named Sam Brannan was the first to spread the word about the gold. He wanted to sell supplies to the miners he knew would come to the area. Soon, California's first newspaper, the *California Star*, was printing stories about it.

By 1849, people were coming from all over the world to California to look for gold. Many arrived first in San Francisco and then headed toward the Sacramento Valley.

The story spread east through letters and newspapers. By August 1848, the news had reached New York and was published in the *New York Herald*. From there, the news traveled to other countries and attracted people from outside the United States. Within a year, people from South America, Europe, and China were traveling to California to find their fortunes.

Gold Fever

Thousands of people were struck with "gold fever." By mid-June 1848, three out of every four men in San Francisco had left to search for gold. In 1849, men called "forty-niners" from every state, as well as other countries, joined the Gold Rush. In all, more than 80,000 forty-niners left their homes, families, and jobs to come to California.

Gold nuggets

The prospectors in this picture are using a pan to look for bits of gold in a river.

By 1853, more than 250,000 people had traveled to California. Most of these **prospectors** were men, but there were women and children, too. The miners included Native Americans who left their villages, soldiers who abandoned their posts, and people from countries as far away as China and Australia.

Coming to California

Most people from the eastern United States traveled to California by sea. They had to sail 15,000 miles (24,140 km) around South America to get to San Francisco. Passengers traveled on dirty, crowded ships for six months or longer. Food often spoiled and water was not always safe to drink. Many people got sick and some died. Others died when their ships sank in storms.

Some people choose to travel 2,000 miles (3,220 km) over land in covered wagons. This trip was also dangerous. People ran out of food and had trouble finding water. Others got lost. Many got sick and died of diseases like **cholera**.

Here is how San Francisco's port looked in the mid-nineteenth century, when many people sailed there to take part in the Gold Rush.

Life in a Mining Camp

Prospectors lived in tents or shacks crowded together in mining camps. Each camp had its own set of rules. Life in the camps was not easy. Fighting, stealing, and **gambling** were common. Mining supplies and food were very expensive. Many prospectors could not make enough money mining to pay for their food. There were no fresh fruits or vegetables. Many miners got sick and died from poor **nutrition** and diseases, like **scurvy**.

This photograph shows the Gold Hill mining camp in California.

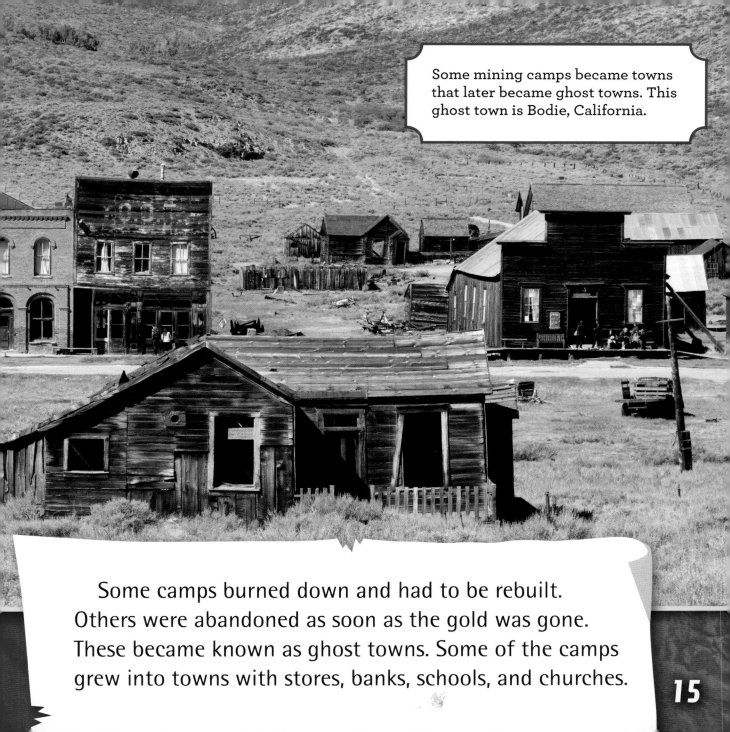

Some mining camps became towns that later became ghost towns. This ghost town is Bodie, California.

Some camps burned down and had to be rebuilt. Others were abandoned as soon as the gold was gone. These became known as ghost towns. Some of the camps grew into towns with stores, banks, schools, and churches.

Searching for Gold

In the early days of the Gold Rush, miners found gold by panning for it. They placed sand and gravel from the bottom of a stream or river into a shallow pan. Then they swished the water around so that the sand and gravel washed over the edges. The heavier gold would be left on the bottom of the pan. Miners squatted in freezing cold water panning for up to 16 hours a day! Later, people began to use machines to mine for gold.

Most miners found only flakes and very small nuggets of gold. Some found no gold at all. A few lucky miners found large chunks.

In this picture, miners are looking for gold in the river using sluice boxes. These are used to separate rocks and dirt from gold.

Striking it Rich

A few prospectors found enough gold to become rich. Stories of their success made others want to keep trying. Although they worked hard, most prospectors were not that lucky. Many miners returned home with nothing. By 1852, about 90,000 people had boarded ships to leave California. Some people stayed in California and found other types of work.

This man is wearing clothes a prospector would have worn to pan for gold. Denim jeans like he is wearing are still worn today!

Some people made money not from finding gold, but from making and selling things that the miners needed. A German immigrant named Levi Strauss opened a dry goods store in San Francisco in 1853. In 1873, Strauss **patented** denim work pants. People still buy Levi jeans today.

A New State

The population of California grew quickly during the Gold Rush. The new settlers wanted and needed law and order. Toward the end of 1849, California elected its first governor and passed a state **constitution**. On September 9, 1850, California became the 31st state.

When California became a state, the 150,000 Native Americans who lived there were not made legal citizens. This meant that they had few **rights**. White Americans raided Native American villages. Many Native Americans were killed. By 1860, there were just 30,000 Native Americans left in California. Anti-foreign laws and taxes made life difficult for people from Mexico and China, too. They also suffered attacks by white settlers.

These men all lived in California during the Gold Rush.

Forever Changed

By 1853, most of the gold that could be found by panning was gone. The Gold Rush was over by 1855.

Although it lasted only a few years, the Gold Rush changed California forever. Many prospectors stayed in California. Some of the towns and businesses that started during the Gold Rush continued to grow. The millions of dollars in gold that was mined from California helped the new state to grow and helped to make the United States one of the richest countries in the world.

As the Gold Rush went on, individuals panning for gold were replaced by groups of people or companies using machines to try to find gold.

GLOSSARY

cholera (KAH-luh-rah) A painful illness of the stomach that causes pain and throwing up.

constitution (kon-stih-TOO-shun) The basic rules by which a country or a state is governed.

gambling (GAM-bling) Betting money on the result of something.

nutrition (noo-TRIH-shun) The act of getting the food that living things need to live and to grow.

patented (PA-tent-ed) Given a document that stops people from copying an invention.

population (pop-yoo-LAY-shun) A group of animals or people living in the same area.

prospectors (PRAH-spek-terz) People who explore an area for minerals, such as gold.

rights (RYTS) Things that everyone should be able to have or do.

sawmill (SAW-mil) A building in which logs are sawed into boards.

scurvy (SKUR-vee) A disease in which the teeth fall out from a lack of fruits and vegetables.

westward expansion (WES-twurd ik-SPANT-shun) The continued growth of the United States by adding land to the west and having settlers move onto it.

INDEX

WEBSITES

Due to the changing nature of Internet links, PowerKids Press has developed an online list of websites related to the subject of this book. This site is updated regularly. Please use this link to access the list: www.powerkidslinks.com/pswe/grush/